EMBRACE THE MACHINE

111 Ways AI Will Change Your Marketing Job

By Nancy A. Shenker
CEO, theONswitch®
With Jim D'Arcangelo

ISBN: 978-0-9827856-2-1

CONTENTS

Think about yourself and your marketing colleagues...

Executives, marketing directors, social media and content generators, designers, analysts, media buyers, agency people, publicists, and event organizers.

One in four will be replaced by a machine within ten years.

It's a fact.

- CEOs say they value technology more than talent.
- Artificial intelligence is estimated to be a $153 billion industry over the next five years.
- Machines are getting faster, smarter, and more accurate in predicting trends and making decisions.

Don't deny that the change is coming.

How can you survive and prosper?

Accept AI, learn about it, and embrace the machine...and then move as fast as you can to earn and keep your position in the new marketing world.

Yours in intelligence,
Nancy (a human, not a bot)

P.S. This book is dedicated to the memories of my little brother Abe and my father (Lewis), who would have loved the AI era. Both tech geeks and inventors/re-inventors, they were my human inspiration in many ways.

CHAPTER 1
The Intro

Embrace the Machine.

What does that mean? I'm not suggesting you hook up with a robot or hug your laptop. Artificial intelligence (AI) is about to change every aspect of business, marketing, and life. The sooner you understand and embrace that fact and the more you learn about AI, the less likely you'll become obsolete.

Your value as a (human) marketer is decreasing by the day!

Sure, that sounds harsh. But here's the reality... 44 percent of global business leaders surveyed by Executive Search Firm Korn Ferry believe the "prevalence of robotics, automation, and artificial intelligence (AI) will make marketers largely irrelevant in the future of work." What's more, 67 percent said, "technology will create greater value in the future than people will."

That doesn't mean leaders don't care about people. They just know machine learning and AI are the keys to better results and lower costs. That's business.

The machine era is not happening next year...in five years...or even ten years.

It's happening NOW, and it has an impact on all of us. It's not an evolution or a revolution. It'll be an invisible tsunami hitting you hard if you're not prepared. Machines are already thinking, processing data, and making decisions.

The Wall Street Journal reports that 69 percent of businesses are currently using or will use AI in the next five years for business analytics, and 53 percent are committed to applying machine learning.

Don't despair. You still have a value. You just need to get smarter and reinvent yourself, working with machines to change the marketing world.

The purpose of this series is to keep you savvy about AI and what it is (and isn't). It will help you understand the facts and trends, and help ensure you remain relevant and employable. You may even discover that AI transforms a boring job into one where you can be the brain while a friendly (and smart) machine performs the tedious tasks for you.

Some of you may have missed the marketing technology revolution. You thought it was a fad. Or, you were busy doing other things. We get it. But AI will have a much bigger impact on our lives and careers than "martech" did.

Of course you could simply Google "AI" and read hundreds of thousands of articles—some fact and some opinion. Or, you could ask Siri or Alexa specific questions.

But I've made your life easier and compiled the best facts and trends into one easy-to-digest list; simple to scan and process. As human attention spans shrink, digesting information in short, telegraphic (and still smart) segments has become more popular.

The sources for this book (including myself) have run businesses, led teams, and been responsible for bottom-line results. We know you want information you can apply, not just theory.

WHY 111?

The reason is simple. The number has significant meaning in numerology (if you're into that kind of thing), and it's binary, yet big. It means the "gates of opportunity are open."

Artificial Intelligence will open up opportunity, but, as noted earlier, it will eliminate more jobs than it will create. You need to find the gate and scramble over it, starting now!

The first few chapters (1-3) are the basics. If you fancy yourself an AI expert, feel free to skip right to Chapter 4, where you'll find more practical and actionable ways to incorporate AI into your marketing and business life.

I've done extensive research and, rather than just bundling a bunch of content with some cool pix, I've added my own commentary and suggestions throughout. As a consultant, writer, and speaker my role is to aggregate, educate, and illuminate. Once you've read the content, you can do what Miss Smith, my 8th grade algebra teacher used to say as we left the classroom: "Take it and make it yours." I never understood what she was talking about until I grew into adulthood. She was simply saying that all an educator can do is give you the tools. They are yours to interpret and incorporate into your life and work.

First, some history...

"Artificial intelligence is that activity devoted to making machines intelligent, and intelligence is that quality that enables an entity to function appropriately and with foresight in its environment." - Nils J. Nilsson

1. Artificial Intelligence is Not a New Concept. It dates back to ancient Greece. The theory that inanimate objects are capable of having "brains" has long been a human belief.

2. When Did People Start Using the Term "Artificial Intelligence?" It was used for the first time in the Summer of 1956 at Dartmouth University during a conference.

3. Science Fiction Writers and Filmmakers Have Had a Long Love Affair with AI. We can all think of movies and books in which smart robots lived among humans (and in some cases overpowered them). But back to reality... researchers have explored AI since the 1950s.

4. Two Eras Are Called the "Winters of AI." From 1974 to the early 1980's, and 1987 to 1993, scientists focused on other pursuits, disillusioned by early failures. LiveScience.com published a great graphic timeline.

5. The Tech Boom Seemed to Awaken Our Interest in AI. When Watson (the IBM-developed computer) won Jeopardy in 2011, people began to take AI seriously. Then the Google Brain was able to recognize cat videos in 2012. Hell—if it happens on television or YouTube, it must be real, right? The mass media and consumers believed maybe a machine really could be as smart (if not smarter) than a human.

6. AI is Booming Now! Over the past few years, new uses for AI are being realized. The speed with which AI is being developed and adopted across industries is rapidly accelerating. Advances in technology and the need for companies to streamline operations are among the contributing factors. Stanford University's 100 Year Study is one of the best academic overviews of the implications of AI for various industries and how we live.

7. Why Start with AI and Marketing?

- I have worked in marketing throughout my career. As a Baby Boomer and digital immigrant, I've seen the industry change rapidly, and watched many colleagues become obsolete because they "missed the memo" about how the world was evolving. We must prepare NOW for the AI-powered jobs of the future, no matter what age we are.
- Marketing jobs are definitely in the high-risk area, in terms of being replaced by machines. As you'll learn in the chapters ahead, attracting and keeping customers—and getting them to love and spend more time with you—is a skill machines are being trained to do.
- Not a marketer? As consumers, we are all touched every day by algorithms that suggest what we should buy, where we should go, and who we should meet. It's a very relatable topic.
- Marketing is all about using actionable information to guide purchase decisions. The better the data, the more we can match the right product to the right person at the right time in the right way. That leads to greater satisfaction—for both business and buyer. In turn, that leads to word-of-mouth marketing and repeat business. And more actionable information. You get the idea. Machines are well equipped to gather and process that data and control that process.

- Because marketers are quite prolific, we had many sources to draw from.

Whether you have made your career in marketing or are simply curious about how marketers are applying artificial intelligence and machine learning, we trust you'll profit from and apply some of these 111 facts and ideas.

Coming soon...more books in the series, each dealing with how a specific industry is being changed by AI, so you can plan your career around where the machines are.

8. Humans Rule (for Now). Remember this important and highly-relevant equation as you read and learn.

No matter how sophisticated and smart machines become, human vision, intervention, judgment, and oversight are critical in ensuring those machines are used to improve the quality of life and data.

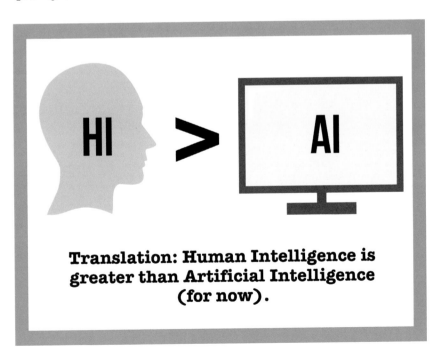

Translation: Human Intelligence is greater than Artificial Intelligence (for now).

Unfortunately, many leaders don't understand this responsibility or don't take it seriously enough. Machines are now slaves to the capabilities of the humans running them.

The organizations who will be left behind in the "rise of the machine" are those who just build and program machines and then walk away. The people who will be left behind are those who don't realize how AI will change their jobs.

"Everything we love about civilization is a product of intelligence, so amplifying our human intelligence with artificial intelligence has the potential of helping civilization flourish like never before – as long as we manage to keep the technology beneficial."
- Max Tegmark, President of the Future of Life Institute

9. How Do We Envision the Business of the Future? It will require a combination of well-oiled smart machines (as it were) to aggregate data and trends and make recommendations on what to do with it. They will be led (or perhaps steered) by a team of experienced, insightful, and flexible humans who will build the next generation of machines, but also review and question the data they spit out, applying our own sense of history and human intelligence. Our guts won't be overridden by machines... they will be augmented by them. For more on what the marketing team of the future needs to look like, see Chapter 6.

10. One Day Soon a Machine Will Write the First Draft of a Book Like This. In fact:

> "Nearly half of all jobs may be automated in a decade."
> -The Economist
>
> "In Marketing, that number may be as high as 25 percent! Be the 75 percent embrace the machine (and read this book!)"
> -Nancy A. Shenker

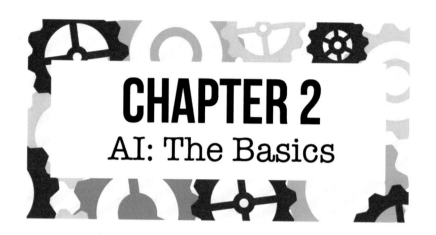

CHAPTER 2
AI: The Basics

11. What is AI? One of the clearest definitions is this one from TechTarget:

AI (pronounced AYE-EYE) or artificial intelligence is the simulation of human intelligence processes by machines, especially computer systems. These processes include learning (the acquisition of information and rules for using the information), reasoning (using the rules to reach approximate or definite conclusions), and self-correction. Particular applications of AI include expert systems, speech recognition and machine vision."

12. What is Machine Learning? Machine learning is a type of AI. It provides computers with the ability to learn without being explicitly programmed. As computers are fed new data, they change how they work and "think."

Beware hype and posers. AI is becoming something of a buzzword, like gluten-free or sustainable. It's been used a lot lately for the cool (or fear) factor. Know your terms and separate the faux artificial from the real artificial intelligence.

13. What Are the Types of AI? We typically hear about four main types of artificial intelligence, as manifested through machines.

- Reactive machines, like a chess-playing computer.
- Limited memory machines. Self-driving cars can process information from the past, but it is not permanently stored or used for future actions.
- Theory of mind machines, who "understand thoughts, emotions, and behaviors."
- Self-awareness machines, who have programmed themselves to be self-conscious. Is that getting too sci-fi for you? A simple experiment in which robots were given the 'wise men' test indicated that robots could develop a sense of self through repeated training.

14. The Definition of AI is Changing, Along with Machine Capabilities. The Simplicable website breaks machines into 33 categories, including artificial stupidity (e.g., the ability of a machine to dumb itself down while playing a game) and committee machine, which is a neural network in which machines can make decisions with other machines (probably more efficiently than human committees.)

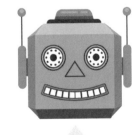

HELLO!

15. The Robots are Coming (or Not). People often think of robots when they hear the words Artificial Intelligence. A robot does not necessarily possess AI. For example, an iRobot Roomba can vacuum your floor, but it doesn't know when your house is dirty and it won't remind you (at least not yet) to make your bed.

16. Weak or Strong? You may hear about two different categories of AI: **Weak AI** is the type of "intelligence" possessed by video game characters or Siri. They seem smart, but are simply designed to repeat pre-programmed tasks. **Strong AI** on the other hand is the ability of a machine to exhibit human qualities, e.g., consciousness, intentionality, self-awareness, creativity, emotional intelligence, problem solving, and reasoning.

17. Robotics and AI are Converging in Many Ways, as developers design "human-like" machines to perform various tasks. The media loves to fuel human paranoia that you'll come back from lunch one day to find a robot sitting in your cubicle or office. One recent article in Quartz led with the headline:

No One is Prepared to Stop the Robot Onslaught. So What Will We Do When it Arrives?
Robots will not attack us with ray guns or fire us from our jobs (yet). Humans build robots to carry out their visions for a better business future. Embrace the robot.

VITAL VOCABULARY SUMMARY

Artificial Intelligence:

The simulation of human intelligence by machines.

Machine Learning:

A type of AI. Computers can be programmed to "behave" differently when exposed to new data.

Robot:

A machine capable of carrying out a complex series of actions automatically, especially one programmable by a computer.

18. A Passing Fad? Nope. If you still doubt AI is here to stay, here's a powerful statistic: The AI industry may grow to well over $150 billion by 2020. That's a lot of machines and talent!

19. Are Marketers Ready? A recent study by media leader Weber Shandwick states that nearly 70 percent of CMOs (Chief Marketing Officers) say their companies are currently selling, using, or planning for business in the AI era. More than half (55 percent) expect AI to have a greater impact on marketing and communications than social media ever had.

20. Who are the Players in the AI Space?
- Researchers and developers.
- Consulting firms, like Accenture and KPMG
- IBM, the creator of Watson and now Project Lucy

- Marketing and PR firms who are hanging out AI shingles and establishing themselves as subject matter experts.
- Close to 700 start-ups who received a whopping $5 billion in funding in 2016, up from $500 million in 2012. These are the companies to watch, as they have received investments of up to $300 million (Israeli-owned transportation app Gett) to build their capabilities.

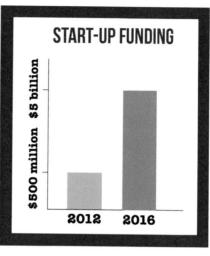

- Nvidia's GPU Ventures program invests in next-generation start-ups in the AI space.
- Amazon, Google, and Facebook (of course!)

21. Brands Embracing the Machine. One might think big consumer brands would be jumping on the AI bandwagon. Adweek recently profiled the five top B2C (business to consumer) players putting AI into practice. They include Starbucks and Lowes, as well as lingerie brand Cosabella, who is applying AI to creative development (see Chapter 4). Amazon and IBM rounded-out the list. Amazon uses its own AI to recommend specific products and re-orders to customers, and is now getting into the business of selling its AI capabilities to other businesses' developers. IBM, the parent of Watson, has teamed-up with Salesforce to build the ultimate customer intelligence system.

22. Artificial Intelligence Will Impact All Aspects of Marketing—from the creative to the analytical... from communication development to customer service. The skills CMOs will need will evolve, as will the roles within their organizations. We can prepare by:

- Getting and staying smart.
- Accepting the fact that AI is inevitable in our industry.
- Embracing the marketing machine rather than denying or fighting it will help ensure you remain employed and viewed as a leader.
- Learning new skills (regardless of your age and position).
- Remembering the role of humans in leadership, talent recognition, and team-building. Perhaps as machines take on more "responsibility" within organizations, human interaction and experience will become even more important. As long as we're selling to and dealing with flesh-and-blood people, we must keep our souls alive and well!

23. One Sure Thing... DATA. We marketers have more of it than ever before. Big data. Lots of data. Data, data, and more data. Each day 2.5 quintillion bytes of data are created; 90 percent of that data was created in just the past two years, according to IBM. Using data to make rational marketing decisions is the core of great marketing, with AI at its epicenter. Humans are already teaching machines what data is most relevant to their businesses and where to find it. The machines will take it from there. Self-service data tools will proliferate.

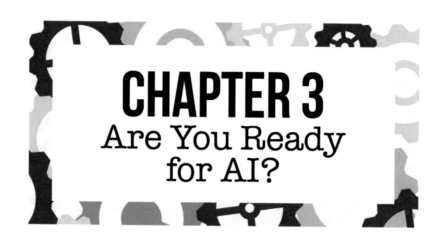

CHAPTER 3
Are You Ready for AI?

24. What Skills Will You Need? You don't need to know how to code to remain relevant in the AI evolution/revolution (although it can't hurt). What will be important is lifelong learning. The nanodegree (short courses that teach specific and just-in-time skills) may start to replace other types of education.

25. You Can Spend More Time Thinking Great Thoughts. The machine takes a seat at the table and can streamline routine tasks, freeing up brain space for you to tackle big new initiatives.

IT'S TIME FOR A QUIZ!

Start by asking yourself:

- What tasks do you do now that could be done by a machine?

- Does that machine or program currently exist?

- What is the cost of buying that tool/software or hiring a developer?

- How much time will you need to invest in training?

- How much time and money will you save short-term? Long-term?

26. Can a Machine Do Your Job? A cool little calculator developed by Oxford University and Deloitte allows you to see—in just a few seconds—whether your job can be automated over the next two decades. (See the Sources for the website, as featured by the BBC)

27. Some Industries will Incorporate AI Sooner than Others. A great graphic cheat sheet from McKinsey outlines which functions will be affected the soonest and most dramatically by AI. Industry trend-watchers predict healthcare, customer service, finance, and insurance will be among the first areas where machines displace manual labor.

In the next few chapters, we'll go through the "classic" steps in the marketing process, and explain how each of them will be changed by AI.

CHAPTER 4
The AI-Powered Marketing World

"Whoever is closest to the consumer controls the conversation. But it's not you who's closest—it's the machines."
- Jason Alan Snyder in Adweek

THE MARKETING PROCESS

This is not sci-fi. You turn on your device... and you'll see up-to-the-second data about how many widgets you sold that day, who you've sold them to, which media performed the best, your cost per sale, a summary of your social media engagement, and what actions need to be taken to boost the

results. In fact, those actions will already be scheduled, so you just need to approve or override them.

Most of this is possible today. People and machines need to just assemble the final puzzle pieces. We've come a long way, but many marketing functions (or dysfunctions) are a jumble of legacy systems, flawed data, and leaders/marketers who are machine-phobic or resistant to change. Add to that the close to 4,000 martech companies and agencies that don't always speak to each other.

Marketing technology is no longer a standalone function. It is informing every step in the marketing ecosystem. The barriers between analytical functions and creative functions have begun to crumble. Although specific functional areas of marketing will continue to exist (like PR and Event Planning), machines will be powering planning, decision-making, and analysis.

Here's a simple chart that shows the basics of how the marketing function has evolved as machines have gotten smarter.

AI EVOLUTION & THE MARKETING FUNCTION

	PRE-MARTECH	THE MARTECH ERA	AI
CUSTOMER PROFILING	Time- and labor-intensive research	Automated surveys	Real-time behaviors (live and online) feed profiles
TARGETING	Trial and error	Cumbersome testing Manual analysis, supported by machines	Instant changes to offers and creative, based on data
ANALYSIS	Manual	Machine-managed	Machines digest and act on data, against your pre-set goals
MARKETING TEAM	Specialized jobs Creative, technical, and data functions segregated	Many positions require digital skills	Machines/ humans fully integrated and collaborative

WHO'S YOUR CUSTOMER?
THE NEW RESEARCH

28. Market Research Companies Will Take on New Shapes, as customer intelligence gathering will simply become part of our day-to-day processes. Machines will capture detailed demographic, attitude, and behavior information on both individuals AND on groups and marketers (and their machine counterparts) will make instantaneous creative, product, pricing, and targeting decisions based on real-time behaviors. Companies like Survata are combining research with ad buying. Stand-alone data without action may become a thing of the past. A place for qualitative research will still exist, to "flesh out" the human aspect of decision-making.

29. Fast Forward, and Deep Customer Data Becomes Highly Forecastable. That means the machine knows what the customer wants and needs, and in what place, time, and price, and marketers can act more quickly on customer insights.

30. Anecdotal Data and On-the-Fly Testing of Small Groups (Via Today's Agile Marketing Systems) will be dark history in the AI marketing world. Customer data will be so rich, so varied, and so current that those data points will seem like irrelevant blips.

31. Predicting Performance of New Products and Services will still require qualitative studies — some done by humans and some machine-facilitated, based on the complexity of the study. Attitudes and outlooks are human (and often quirky) factors, so marketers will still need to dig a little deeper before drawing conclusions.

32. Personas will Soon be Dead. We will laugh in ten years about the old days of constructing buyer personas (clusters of users who exhibit similar behavioral patterns). Today, they are created using more traditional research and analysis, and third party demographic data. AI will automate and update customer data. Companies like Mariana (a data analytics firm) are using social media behavioral data as an overlay to develop more specific buyer personas. They claim to sift through 50k data points and 5TB (that's terabytes) of data. Tools like Swarm AI feed consumer sentiment data into the machines as well, replacing polls with instantaneous trend tracking, increasing our knowledge of groups and individuals.

33. It's Elementary, Watson! More than 550 companies across 17 industries (including marketing companies) are utilizing IBM's Watson and Lucy technologies to aggregate and decipher data. Marketing agencies, realizing old-school research and media buying services may be dying a rapid death, are getting into the data aggregation and presentation business. Using machines rather than number-crunching associates, they are able to identify and share consumer trends and behaviors in record time.

SERVING UP A BETTER CUSTOMER EXPERIENCE WITH AI

34. Do Consumers Think Brands Know a Little TOO Much About Them? Amazon suggests what they should read, watch, or buy. Waze urges them to pull off the road at the stop they're approaching to get a doughnut and coffee, while Spotify suggests the next track they'd like. The reality is that although consumers are worried about job loss to machines, more than 50 percent of people surveyed in a recent study trust machines to make product recommendations, and believe they make their lives easier.

35. The Golden Age of Consumer Insight and Intelligence Has Just Begun. Watson is now working with 45+ consumer brands to serve up value-added content and customized product suggestions ranging from Campbell's soup recipes (based on the ingredients you have in your house) to personalized learning for kids.

36. As Every Great Marketer Knows... marketing is all about attracting the right new prospects, giving them the right offer, at the right place and time, through the right medium. That encourages them to engage with you and ultimately make a purchase. The buyer consideration stage, purchase continuum, and customer lifecycle are all connected today. Soon, with the help of AI they will evolve with speed, accuracy, ease, and invisibility. In the AI world, processes will be driven at least 75 percent by machines. Marketers will just fill in the cracks (so to speak).

37. AI Will Improve Communications—Between Machines! A challenge many marketers face today is the integration of multiple systems. As you can imagine, with 5,000 different solutions, training machines to "talk to each other" requires time, resources, and human intervention (today). As the world of marketing technology consolidates and machines get smarter, these integrations will become simpler. Marketing systems will talk to sales systems directly and seamlessly, and optimize even more quickly. Smart companies will buy other "tech stack" companies and offer integrated solutions to their enterprise customers. The space will consolidate, because not all 4,000 can afford to get into and master the high stakes world of AI.

38. A/B and AI: Every seasoned marketer has been through rounds of creative and message testing (as in A/B testing.) As AI becomes more sophisticated, machines will instantly read results and make immediate adjustments based on effectiveness—even down to the level of which creative approach seems to be working with a specific market segment. The lines between technology and creative are blurring and, as you'll learn as you read on, machines are capable of creating content (words and design) that will feed automatically into the AI-powered targeting system.

39. Targeting by Medium Will be a Thing of the Past. In the world of AI, the machine will know which channels work with which customer, how to bid for paid search, and how each customer likes his or her new offers presented. Machines will not only select media channels, but they will also decide which channels work best together, and in which sequence. Biggest data (way beyond the big data of today) will choose targets and deliver the right offers at the right time of day. AI will make the media decisions for the marketing team, and recommend spending levels.

40. Offers and prices will be optimized across all products. In other words pricing, features, and even colors will be personalized, based on unprecedented depths of data, harnessed to meet each buyer's wants and needs—in real time.

Airlines have been driven by big data for years. Success is reflected in high seat occupancy and record profits.

41. Beyond the Phone—the IoT. Your phone is not the only device that knows where you are and what you're doing. The Internet of Things (IoT) refers to any device—like a wearable fitness tracker—that knows your behaviors and preferences. These devices also "communicate" with other smart devices, creating a useful web of aware things; These things will understand, interpret, and extrapolate our needs. For example, your refrigerator will "know" that you're low on yogurt and will order your favorite brand without your asking. Two-thirds of consumers own an IoT device, and 65 percent of them are actually interested in receiving marketing messages on the device, according to the Interactive Advertising Bureau, as reported by GeoMarketing.

42. Snow is in the Forecast...the Machine Knows What You Should Do! In a review of how location-based marketing will evolve, one marketer predicts, "Weather, location, and consumer confidence measures will quickly become married to stored customer and transaction data. Sophistication in location, in particular, will form the basis of better and more impactful targeting and useful triggers for media placements and execution." In other words, using artificial intelligence, brands will know whether you're a homebody who likes to stock-up on canned goods before a blizzard, or if you're an avid skier who can't wait to hit fresh powder. Messages and offers will be served-up to your device before the first snowflake falls.

43. When AI is King, Content May Have to Change its Crown. AI will lead to auto-generated content across all media. It's already used by media as large as Associated Press and as small as GameChanger. More on that later......

44. We As Consumers Have an Obligation to Make Machines Smarter. Amazon attributes a 29 percent sales increase to its algorithm-generated recommendations. Yet, they can be very robotic (and sometimes even annoying.) For example, I looked TWICE at an item to give away as a trade show gift. Now, every time I log-in to my Amazon account I see multiple images of that tchotchke (swag). I have no intention of ever buying it. I was just window shopping, yet the machine thinks my two-time view indicated interest. Another great example is my recent trip to Disney. I bought a stuffed Pooh bear and chocolate bars as gifts, so I'm now on the "she bought merchandise, so she must want more" list for customer nurture and cross-sell. I'm not faulting either of these brands (or their machines) for drawing conclusions. The point is...the more we provide feedback to companies when given the opportunity, the better the job they'll do in recommending products and making our lives simpler. As time-consuming as it is, I keep providing Google with feedback on my smart phone pop-up ads. I have an obligation to teach the machine.

45. Customer Feedback Will Shape Brands and Inform the Machine. Creative strategy and execution (which we'll cover in the sections ahead) will be shaped by every customer interaction—from Yelp and product reviews to online bot conversations. Subjective agency presentations and management biases will still exist, but may be overruled by data. The machine will be a brand champion of sorts.

46. What Else Can You Do as a Marketer? Marketers at all levels should serve as both AI experts and evangelists, staying current and leading the change. You can help management understand AI and encourage and educate team members.

The number of AI sessions at marketing conferences are bound to multiply. It's a star at conferences like SXSW and Collision. Big vendors like Salesforce, Marketo, and others host national gatherings, and you can learn best practices from the brands and business marketers who are ahead of the curve. Mid-level managers should also pursue accreditation in a specific area. (Examples of these types of programs HubSpot Academy and Salesforce Certification.) Some general courses are listed at the back of this guide as well. Beware of overpriced scams or classes in technologies that may be obsolete in a year or two.

CONTENT

47. The Traditional Creative Director and Agency Model is a Thing of the Past in the AI World. Although creative people still drive the process of combining words and pictures, they will be informed by machines who give them feedback on what's creating the most awareness and sales. (We are already moving quickly down this path. Facebook can easily tell me which color background and type of post has generated the most engagement. I don't even need to ask the question.)

Machines have already been proven capable of creating. But can they produce masterpieces, or imagine bold and unique concepts on their own? The jury is out on this one. My technology friends say, "Absolutely!" My artist friends say, "Kill me before that happens!" I can only say, "We'll see."

One thing is certain: Automation has transformed the creative process. Whereas a company may need five people to create content today, that number may drop to one or two tomorrow. How do you ensure you're the last man (or woman) standing?

48. The Robot Publisher? Writers and creative types are sometimes appalled when the topic of machine-generated content or graphics comes up. We like to believe great words and pictures can only be compiled by people with flesh, blood, and soul. The reality is that much of marketing writing today

relies on assembling facts, insights, and keywords, and compiling them in a way that makes sense. Several AI systems are already in development that compile content, and they are being used by major news organizations.

49. Content Marketing is the Lifeblood of Lead Generation for many businesses and if they can find a way to do more of it, faster and better, they will have put machines to good use. (By the way, content marketing is the creation and sharing of blogs, social media posts, videos, and other tidbits of knowledge and entertainment that does not directly promote a brand, product, or service, but is intended to stimulate interest and build credibility.)

50. Welcome to the Natural Language Generation! NLG as it's often called is the ability of a machine to create content, based on human direction. At least it requires human direction today. In the future, machines may direct other machines. Narrative Science.com offers a terrific explanation of the different types of NLG.

51. Where Does NLG Stand Today? You may already be reading content created by a machine. Large companies have started using NLG tools to create stories for their media outlets. NLG works best for factual content, where human emotion and humor are not required. However, the machines of the future will, most likely, be trained to make you cry or laugh.

52. The NLG Players. Wordsmith is one of the established NLG companies. At $2,000/month, they target primarily enterprise-level businesses. Associated Press (AP) publishes 3,000 financial reports each quarter using the Wordsmith platform.

53. Tell Me a Story. Another NLG platform called Quill uses data to create what they call "intelligent narratives." One of their products takes Google Analytics data and processes it into a cogent presentation—ready to take to a client or CMO.

54. Presentation Jitters No More! Today, we sweat over creating PowerPoints and Prezis. AI technologies have been in-the-works since 2010, and many start-ups have joined Google and Amazon in the development of machine-generated ways to compile and share stories and data on the big screen for presentations. As *Fast Company* declared, "If the all-too-familiar death-by-PowerPoint experience so many of us suffer is finally headed to a grave of its own, it may be a machine that puts it there." Haiku Deck, Zuru, and SlideBot are among the start-ups who are entering this highly-competitive space.

55. Think About It and the Machine Says It. Telepathy is not as far away as you may think, thanks to Elon Musk and Mark Zuckerberg. Musk's company Neuralink is developing ways for people's brains to communicate with machines without speech. Not only will this be a tremendous help for people who have suffered brain injuries, it will eventually transform the entire process of utilizing keyboards to create content. Facebook is also developing similar technologies, to shortcut the brain-to-screen transition.

56. What are the Advantages of Machines Writing Content? Hours of research time will be saved finding just the right sources for a blog or news story. Assuming machines are checking and rechecking data, statistics and trends will be accurate and easy to find.

57. Finding the Right Words. Today, many sources exist that enable content writers to pepper their stories with popular keywords. In fact, some marketers choose their topics based solely on most-searched terms. Machines will make finding the most-searched terms faster and simpler, and they will also be able to quickly identify trends as they are breaking, enabling smart marketers to stay one step ahead of the curve.

SOCIAL MEDIA AUTOMATION

58. Where Does This Section Fit? Is social media purely a marketing activity? Is it a relationship-development strategy? It involves martech AND content AND graphic design (plus, sub-specialties like video). Can it be controlled entirely by marketing machines, or is it more human-powered than machine-powered? Not to be wishy-washy, but the answer is definitely "It depends."

It depends on whether the objective is marketing/sales or relationship development. *VentureBeat* outlines the ways in which social media will streamline marketing tasks by finding trending topics, separate bots from people, identify influencers, analyze post types and frequency, and much more. They call it "Social Artificial Intelligence."

59. Post for Me, Bots! In the early days of social media, posting on the various sites was a highly manual and tedious process. Big brands filled cube farms with interns and recent grads posting and tweeting. Additional seats were filled with media buyers and analysts who looked at the data, and made recommendations on what to expand and what to kill. Then automation tools like Hootsuite made pre-posting and analysis easier and faster. But the AI wave is just beginning in social media.

60. The Times are Changing (Literally). *The New York Times* is already using AI to manage its social media pages—300 posts a day, in fact. According to *VentureBeat*, "the intelligent bot helps predict how stories will perform on social media, as well as suggests which stories editors should boost or promote the posts generated by the chatbot received almost 380 percent more clicks."

61. Making Friends & Influencing People. If you're thinking about turning your entire LinkedIn profile and connection process over to AI tomorrow, the world is not quite ready for that. Relationship-building is in human hands today, assisted by machines. Ask me again in a couple of years. I can definitely imagine a world in which humans have independent "trust scores" based on past behaviors, and facial scanning will inform me if a potential client or business partner is "shifty-eyed."

THE MACHINE AS AN ARTIST

62. Machines Can Paint and Draw. That's old news already. AI artist PIX18 has its portfolio of paintings on a website. I won't be hanging any of them on my apartment walls, but I'm still impressed by the quality; indistinguishable from the work of some human painters. Machines can also now score music and produce videos and animations.

63. HERE'S A CHALLENGE

One element in this book was designed by a machine (via an AI-enabled design program). Can you find it?

64. Machine-Assisted Graphic Design is Nothing New. Photoshop and other graphic programs have been used by designers for years to render the images in their brains. As consumers, we now take for granted tools like Instagram filters, template website builders, design programs like Canva, and GIF- and meme-generators. The paintbrush has been replaced in many cases by the keystroke or swipe.

65. Now Let's Take it One Step Further... The Grid and Wix ADI have both been around for a while, applying machine learning to web design. Their algorithms enable testing of various layouts, an extremely valuable feature for marketers. In the future, subjective creative debates will be minimized because the machine will tell us what works best.

66. The Naked Truth? Luxury lingerie brand Cosabella applied AI to its web catalog creation, and according to Adweek, the results were impressive. For example, "Switching the color of a button on a checkout page to pink increased conversions for a product by 34.9 percent." Cosabella's sales overall have increased 35.6 percent, thanks to AI. Six months of testing was reduced to 30 days.

67. Machine: Make Me a Logo! AI-powered Logojoy (which has produced close to 3 million logos to date) can "produce designs just like a designer would." However, one of the options they offer on their site is a one-hour session with a human being. Perhaps the eye is still more powerful than the keyboard!

68. Test the AI Designer—FREE! Simply enter your company name into MarkMaker™, a free logo generator, and the machine will create variations. Indicate which ones you like and you'll get specific ideas based on your taste. Co.Design is underwhelmed and declared, "bots are still pretty crap at design."

Harsh... but I have to agree. However, for start-ups and small businesses these technologies present a cool alternative to human-powered design options.

69. Machines are Learning How to Write Captions. Google's captioning AI is supposedly 94 percent accurate, but it's not available to the general public right now so I couldn't

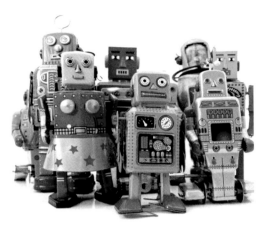

test it. Microsoft's CaptionBot is clearly still in its development and education phase. I challenged it to caption this image from Shutterstock (one of my faves) and it responded with, "I am not really confident, but I think it's a group of toy doll."

Note that it doesn't yet recognize plurals and is honest enough to express uncertainty. I was able to provide feedback, and I'm certain it will learn from it. That experience just proves machines need us humans to get smarter.

70. Doodle Me This! If you have 20 seconds to spare, you can challenge the machine to recognize your doodle on the beta Quickdraw.withgoogle.com. Sadly, it thought my monkey was a bear and my toilet sketch was a potato, which is probably more a statement about my drawing ability and the beta version of the machine learning than about AI in general. Google has since perfected its art recognition capabilities and AutoDraw has replaced the earlier version. The company is smart in that it's involving users in "training the machine."

"To stand the test of time, graphic designers will need to focus on steering the creative direction instead of doing the actual creation bringing big picture ideas and customized components to designs . While the creation process may shift, human engagement between designers and their clients to bring projects to life will become increasingly important."
- Anna Osgoodby, Graphic Designer at Bold & Pop

71. Harvard Says... A recent Harvard Business Review article reveals the results of a study published in AIEDAM (Artificial Intelligence for Engineering Design, Analysis, and Manufacturing.) It found the fastest modern supercomputer couldn't list or explore all the features of an object/thing - even if it had started working on the problem way back in the 1950s. The conclusion is that "there will always be limits to how creative a computer can be." Always is a pretty strong word, but the point of the article is that humans need to work WITH computers to guide them and fill in the creative gaps. They propose the development of an interface that makes that possible.

"Computers, for example, could prevent humans from falling prey to cognitive biases such as functional fixedness, design fixation, goal fixedness, assumption blindness, and analogy blindness. And humans could make up for the creative deficiencies of computers. In order for this to work, the interface needs to be both human- and computer-friendly."
- Tony McCaffrey in HBR

PR & MEDIA RELATIONS

72. In Denial or Late Adopters? Fewer than 3 percent of the many media stories about AI mention the words "public relations," according to a writer in PR News. Are PR professionals simply consumed with covering developments in the field, but failing to see how it might impact their own world? Technology is impacting every aspect of how real (and fake) news gets disseminated. At some point soon, AI will leave a mark on PR.

73. Who's the Media? Although conventional news outlets like television, radio, and print still exist, six in ten

Americans get their news via social media, according to Pew Research. Citizen journalists abound, and news outlets are as likely to feature an eyewitness' smartphone video as they are a professionally-produced segment. The day is near when a machine will identify a news story and instantly deploy a drone to shoot and transmit footage (which can then be captioned by a machine).

74. The Machine is a Journalist. You may not realize that many media outlets have already begun to integrate AI into the newsroom. As noted earlier, media giants like *The New York Times* and Associated Press are already using AI to generate content. The *New York Post* has been using Heliograph to generate news stories, as has the *Washington Post*. Their AI will even alert human journalists via Slack when it finds anomalies in data.

75. What's the Big Story? Whether the topic is medical advances, fashion trends, or the death of a celebrity, reporters and writers are able to identify trending topics, assisted by machines. They gather sources at the same time public relations agencies and professionals are feeding new bits and bytes of information. Artificial intelligence will speed-up and streamline this process. Media outlets (utilizing AI) will instantly scan the web for trending or leading topics, and PR professionals will "feed the machine" with expert quotes and facts.

76. The Robot Research Assistant. An AI-driven tool called JUICE is in development by Google, specifically for news writers. As a journalist creates a story, AI will assist him or her with relevant sources.

77. The Press List of the Future. PR professionals are already using simple AI in their day-to-day lives. Once they identify a category for their stories, programs like Cision and Meltwater locate media and influencers. The number of machine-enabled companies in this space has expanded in recent years. According to Hubspot, at least 18 "media identifiers" are now available.

78. Will People Still Need to Pitch? Perhaps. Imagine a world where PR pros will simply introduce their news bots to each other over coffee and cocktails. As in all other aspects of marketing, humans still add a trust and relationship component to business. However, for some tasks (like pitching speakers or posting expert profiles, bots may be self-sufficient one day soon!

LIVE EVENTS

79. Machine-Powered Consumer Festivals and Trade Shows are certainly possible. Databases of talent, temporary workers, and potential exhibitors will all be easily accessible in the future. Smart machines will match availability and geography with the right sponsors and attendees. We're already seeing apps integrated into most large-scale events, and some organizers even use geotargeting to direct attendees to booths and features (like Waze for trade show guests.)

80. Facial and Fingerprint Recognition Technology is already in use at Disney properties, along with wearable technology (a $1 billion investment by the brand, according to *Wired*). Next on Disney's agenda for their theme parks: AI-powered robot characters.

81. How Else will AI Impact Live Events?
A great infographic from EventMB outlines other ways AI may be integrated into the events industry, changing everything from advertising and invitations, through security, to customer service and follow-up.

PURCHASING

82. Meet the Robot Purchasing Agent! Today, we rely on word-of-mouth recommendations (either live or powered by LinkedIn or other social media) when looking for service providers. If you work at a large company, your purchasing or finance department is involved in the process. Going forward, procurement of goods and services will be AI-powered. You'll identify what goods or services you're looking for, and your purchasing machine will tell you who the best vendors are and why.

83. The Robot Writes Your RFP Response! If you work for an agency or service provider, you can kiss cutting-and-pasting goodbye. The machine will identify key words in RFPs and match them up to your company's capabilities, assessing the competition and generating comparative charts. The response will, most likely, be reviewed by a machine on the other end. What about the role of inter-company chemistry? We believe that although some of those factors can be evaluated via AI, people who work together must still like and trust each other. As with online dating, an algorithm can only take a relationship so far.

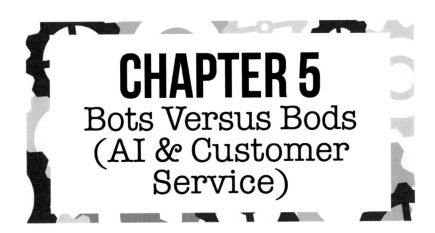

CHAPTER 5
Bots Versus Bods (AI & Customer Service)

84. How Can I Help You? Whether you are shopping or buying services in real life or on a website, the level of service you get contributes to your experience of a brand. A whopping 64 percent of consumers believe companies should be using bots (or some form of automated communication) to answer basic questions.

85. But All Bots are Not Created Equal. Just because a bot can answer a question, that doesn't immediately mean customer satisfaction. Of the 60 percent of millennials who say they've interacted with bots, 21 percent reported having had negative experiences. An overview from *Street Fight* also offers up advice from experts on ways companies can make bot service more human and trustworthy.

86. "Customer Service Needs the Human Touch."
That's the title of a comprehensive article from *HuffPost*. By 2020, 79 percent of customers expect a company to already know who they are when they contact them, and 67 percent expect service to be delivered via virtual reality.

87. Behind-the-Scenes Bots Improve Human Interaction. A "hybrid solution" for delivering great customer service involves AI supporting human reps. This is also 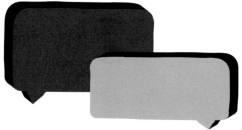 called "cyborg" or "human in the loop." Eight out of ten companies have already incorporated some type of AI into their customer service delivery, according to Oracle.

88. Einstein Lives. Applying customer data to delivering better customer service is one of the main objectives of Salesforce, whose AI initiative is named after you-know-who. They introduced the latest version of their CRM (customer relationship management) tool this year and, as expected, it's still a baby genius, as users provide input to make the tool smarter. Smaller companies are entering this space as well, and as with all technical development, users will end up choosing providers based on quality AND price. AI is still geared for enterprise-level businesses, and the little guy will have to wait a while to enjoy some of the more intelligent AI solutions.

89. The Customer (Not the Bot) is Always Right. As you move towards incorporating AI into your customer service strategy, be sure to weight the time- and cost-savings against the customer benefit. We've all heard (and experienced) horror stories when we've repeated ourselves over and over (and over) again to a voice recognition bot. Be sure whatever solution you embrace is also one your customers will love. Finding new customers (no matter how smart your AI is) is always harder and more expensive than keeping your current customers satisfied.

CHAPTER 6
The New CMO
& His/Her Team

90. Why is This Chapter So Important? Every new technology creates new job opportunities, but AI by its very nature can result in the streamlining or obsolescence of marketing roles. *Forbes* included marketing on its "top 10" list of positions at risk as a result of big data.

91. What's the One-Word Secret That Will Keep a Machine from Stealing Your Job? Augmentation, according to Tom Davenport in this Wall Street Journal article. "Specifically, individuals and organizations need to begin to address *augmentation*—how humans can augment the work of smart machines, and vice versa.

> **As with any position, the key to survival is understanding what's coming, embracing it, and and helping your organization to evolve.**

There has been little thought devoted to this issue thus far; work has been treated as something that can be done by computers or people, but not both." Marketo offers up great tips on how you can "robot-proof" your marketing job.

92. Who's the New CMO? Being a strong leader and understanding the value of a brand is so yesterday. Today's and tomorrow's Chief Marketing Officer (CMO) needs to also be exceptionally tech-friendly and data-savvy. No matter what the industry, he/she needs to understand (and embrace) how technology can streamline and improve every aspect of the role—especially as it relates to customer intelligence. Recruiters and HR departments will also need to rise to the occasion (assisted by machine-generated keywords, perhaps) to find this rare combination of big vision, big data management, and big ability to flex as the speed of machine-powered marketing picks up.

I don't believe organizations should hire separate CAIOs (Chief Artificial Intelligence Officers) as some consultants and writers have proposed. If AI is to be integrated into organizations, it needs to be a major component of everyone's job description. That said, hiring a freelance strategic AI evangelist/consultant to expedite the process, is probably a great idea. (My e-mail address is nancys@theonswitch.com. Even a machine would feel compelled to insert a call to action at this point in content.)

93. What Does the New AI-Driven Marketing Ecosystem Look Like? Here's my best guess of what a marketing department of the future will look like. These are not intended to be exact job titles. "The Technical Team" is also a pretty broad category. What we do know is that within the next 10 years, every member of a marketing department or agency will need to be familiar with machines and their capabilities, and will use them in their daily lives to get stuff done.

Marketing departments and functions are continuously evolving. Just think about how much companies and agencies have changed in the past five years. For example, the terms "content marketing" and "marketing automation" were barely spoken a few short years ago. Today, every major consumer brand has a content strategy and marketing automation conferences are attended by close to 10,000 professionals and the media.

Every marketing team member's function will be augmented or taken over by AI and machine learning. Data and insights are instant and ever-changing. As machines process and digest this data, they'll act on it. We will need to move faster, more intelligently, and collaboratively to use the insights we have at our disposal. Just as customers today demand better and different products, marketers will demand new types of machines and functionality to make their brands and businesses stronger.

Human intervention in the future will take the form of functions that require counsel, psychology, and strategy.

THE MARKETING TEAM OF THE FUTURE: WHAT WILL WE DO?

	TODAY	THE NEAR-TERM (3-5 YEARS)	THE FUTURE (10+ YEARS)
STAFF SIZE	Multiple people within each function	Flat to today but roles shift dramatically	Staff reduced 25%
THE CEO	• Marketing vision • Brand oversight • Customer lifestyle marketing • Customer intimacy • Competitive savvy • Analytics • Team development/leadership/training	• Marketing vision • Brand integration and highly personalized customer marketing (based on customer intelligence) • Spending and competitive strategy based on machine-supplied data • Tough decisions regarding team structure; evolution to machines well underway	• Marketing vision • Brand and customer optimization based on immediate machine-supplied data • Leadership definition changes as staff size comes down
THE TEAM	Organized by specialty: • Content • Digital (paid & organic) • Marketing automation & analytics • Product marketing • Events • PR • Creative • Developers	Beginning of evolution to "machine-assisted" functions: • Content curation • Analytics & data scientists • Cross-platform creative (video, print, digital, social – all machine-assisted) • Machine-assisted events • Machine-assisted PR • Developers	Machines take the lead in all aspects of marketing: • Marketing psychologists (brand and customer stewards) • Content counsel (replaces multiple functions) • Marketing system engineers (replace automation and analytics functions) • Analytics and data scientist • Creative automation strategists (replace graphic designers and many creative directors) • Machine-assisted events (still attended by humans) • Digital publicists and media

94. Man (and Woman) Versus Machine. We all just have to be careful that as this brave new AI world evolves, human instinct and gut (not to mention compassion) do not totally vanish. People need to check  data to ensure it makes sense. Robot-generated stories will lack flesh and blood perspective and emotion. Photographs that evoke emotion still require a human eye. And even if a bot organizes job applications and resumes and visually scans each candidate's profile pictures and videos, you'll still need to be the final screen of character and personality. After all, even in the AI world, no one wants to work with a jerk.

CHAPTER 7
How to Stay Smart

95. By the Time This Book is Published, it May be Out of Date. Such is the nature of the AI space. The links throughout the book are great sources of facts, figures, and perspectives. My goal has been to give you a quick-read recap of what's happening with AI and marketing, and inspire you to stay smart on your own.

96. Know the Lingo. Here are some basic vocabulary words you need to know, beyond the ones we've included throughout the book. And yes, we're sort of cheating because we're counting each one as its own tip.

WORDS TO KNOW

97. Agent: Software programs that can ask questions, respond to commands, pay attention to users' work patterns, serve as a guide and a coach, take on owners' goals, and use reasoning to fabricate their own goals. Source: Quizlet

98. Algorithm: A set of instructions designed to perform a specific task. This can be a simple process, such as basic math, or a complex operation, such as analyzing a social media campaign or e-mail marketing test.

99. Turing Test: Developed by Alan Turing in 1950, it is a test of a machine's ability to exhibit intelligent behavior that is indistinguishable from a human. The BBC published a great perspective on the history and future of the Turing Test.

WHERE TO GO

100. One Day, in the Not-so-Distant Future... You'll simply wake up in the morning and your AI-powered robot guide will read you a carefully curated summary of what's new, and tell you very specifically how you need to act on it. Or perhaps, the machine will have already taken those actions and give you a quick update. Then you can go back to sleep. In the meantime, here are some sites you should check out:

101. Accenture: This site covers a wide variety of topics. Simple, colorful, and highly-readable.

102. Ditto for **AI Trends**: The Business and Technology of AI.

103. You can download **Practical Artificial Intelligence for Dummies** free Narrative Science edition.

104. Intel is clearly jockeying to be a major player in the AI space. Not only have they bought a ton of ad space on Google, they introduced something they call the **Intel® Nervana™ AI Academy**... It seems to be geared more toward developers and academics. Hmmm... are the professors all robots?

105. Speaking of bots, **TopBots** is a marketing and media firm specializing in chatbots. Their site includes some interesting content, presented in human-speak.

106. Want to go "back to school?" Check out **Coursera** for an intro class in Machine Learning from Stanford University.

107. Or, peruse an online AI course catalog from **Class Central.**

108. Add your name to theONswitch list and you'll be notified as new books in this series are published.
Prefer Human Events? Check These Out!

109. aiworld conference and Expo

110. O'Reilly Artificial Intelligence Conference

Last but not least......

111. What better way to end the list than with a quote from one of the believers in artificial intelligence—Isaac Asimov.

"It is change, continuing change, inevitable change, that is the dominant factor in society today. No sensible decision can be made any longer without taking into account not only the world as it is, but the world as it will be."
- Isaac Asimov

CHAPTER 8
Just For Fun

In case reading about how AI could change your job stressed you out, here are some interesting and entertaining places to go and things to do.

Fave Movies About AI

- **2001: A Space Odyssey,** in which Hal the intelligent machine turns evil. Stanley Kubrick did extensive research on AI to create his 1968 masterpiece. Wired.com shares more behind-the-scenes facts. .

- **Ex Machina** also features evil robots. But it features evil humans too. So it all evens out.
- Some bots are heroes. **RoboCop** (the 1987 original, not the remake) is a kitchy but action-packed film.

- They aren't all accurate, but they are fun and provocative. CNET offers even more human-powered reviews of AI films.
- The Brain Center at Whipple's is a great 1964 Twilight Zone episode in which a CEO replaces his workforce with machines...with consequences.
- Captain Kirk of **Star Trek** replaced by a machine? We don't like that idea much either. Nor did he! Find out what happens on the Starship Enterprise in "The Ultimate Computer" episode -- a 1968 glimpse into machine learning and AI.

Passionate About Robots?

- At **The Robot Shop** you can build or buy your own.
- Assuming you still have a desk in the future, you can decorate your workspace with some cool retro robot accessories from **Retroplanet.com**.

ABOUT THE AUTHOR

NANCY A. SHENKER

Nancy A. Shenker is a human agent of change, who has fearlessly embraced the machine. Starting her career in the 1970s, she has always led marketing and creative transformations through technology.

The Founder & CEO of theONswitch marketing consultancy, she held marketing leadership positions at companies including Citibank, Mastercard, and Reed Exhibitions (producers of Comic Con). Nancy has consulted 100's of B-to-B and B-to-C companies, including consumer products, SaaS, real estate, luxury products, and many others.

She speaks at national and local conferences on a wide range of topics, related to innovation, content strategy, digital marketing, cross-generational communications, and women's empowerment.

A contributor to *HuffPost*, she is also the co-author of a career guide for young women (Don't Hook Up With the Dude in the Next Cube), and two business comic books. She has been featured in business and consumer media, including *Forbes*, *Bloomberg BusinessWeek*, *The New York Times*, *The Wall Street Journal*, and many others.

A graduate of the University of Michigan, she has completed graduate work at NYU and Kellogg's Executive Communication program.

When she's not writing, speaking, or consulting, she likes to discover new gadgets, ride her bike, and bake.

Contact her at nancys@theonswitch.com

JIM D'ARCANGELO

Jim was an invaluable strategic advisor, muse, and sounding board throughout this project. He also contributed the forward-thinking content in the "Customer Experience" section.

A leader in the tech startup space, he has spent 20+ years leading growth-stage companies' marketing groups, with three successful exits, and two more on their way. Jim had a hand in the front edge of every tech wave of the last 30 years: the first PCs, online advertising, on-demand movies and video, Internet/e-commerce measurement, mobile content, SaaS, big data, martech, and now AI.

Jim has won a dozen awards between 2015 and 2017 for prospect and client engagement results and marketing automation, tech stack, AI, and analytics, including 2017 Top 33 Marketing Ops Pros, 2016 "Marketing Executive of the Year" PR & Marketing Excellence, and 2016 Marketo Revvie Award finalist, among their 5,000 clients, in the "Marketing Executive of the Year" category. He was selected to give his perspective on machine learning and AI in marketing on *VentureBeat's* VB Live webinar.

A graduate of Princeton University, he holds an MS-Marketing from Johns Hopkins University, and an MBA from George Washington University, where he also conducted doctoral work in Organization Development.

GRATITUDES

I decided to write this book on April 7th, 2017. The research and draft were completed 13 days later. The first "edition" came to life on May 10th, 2017. That's 33 days from start to finish—a little over 4 weeks.

I started my career in the publishing industry. The average lead time back then to produce a book was about 18 months.

The world has sped up and transformed, with an assist from machines.

But one thing hasn't changed: smart, kind, trustworthy, capable humans helping other humans to get stuff done.

Special thanks go to:
- Anna Osgoodby of Bold & Pop. When I told her the timeline for the book, she didn't freak out. In addition to her awesome creative style, that's why I love working with her. Our relationship is a model of millennial/Boomer collaboration!
- Nicky Pomije was my first friend in Minneapolis and continues to serve as an amazing sounding board and inspiration. Her humor gets me through the darkest (and coldest) days.
- Emily Cornell graciously volunteered to read the manuscript and provide honest and just-in-time feedback.
- Phyllis Kaelin was referred to me via my social media network. I learned everything I needed to know from her about ISBNs, Kindle formatting, justification (as in formatting, not as in rationalizing), and so much more. Better than any FAQ by a long-shot!
- Let's train interns for the jobs of tomorrow (ensuring they WILL have jobs.) Thank you to Haley Madderom

and Cindy Simba, who juggled proofreading and indexing with finals season...well done, ladies!

- The machine-driven systems and great companies that helped me write this book—Microsoft, Lenovo, Samsung, and Google. I was able to write and share from anywhere, any time. Thanks also to Booking.com and OpenTable for fueling my travel and refreshment needs as I journeyed throughout my writing time.
- Last but not least, my mom, my daughters, and my grandgirl— strong females all—who love and challenge me...and who will never ever be replaced by robots!

SOURCES

Size of AI market: https://www.techemergence.com/valuing-the-artificial-intelligence-market-2016-and-beyond/

Chapter 1

Korn Ferry survey on the value of technology:
http://www.kornferry.com/press/korn-ferry-global-study-majority-of-ceos-see-more-value-in-technology-than-their-workforce/

Businesses currently using technology: https://www.wsj.com/articles/how-artificial-intelligence-will-change-everything-1488856320

Meaning of 111: http://numerologysecrets.net/numerology-111-meaning/

Nils Nilsson: http://ai.stanford.edu/~nilsson/

AI history:
https://whatsthebigdata.com/2017/02/12/a-very-short-history-of-artificial-intelligence-ai/

AI timeline:
http://www.livescience.com/images/i/000/069/621/original/timeline-of-artificial-intelligence-history-ai-140812f-02.jpg

IBM Watson: http://www.techrepublic.com/article/ibm-watson-the-inside-story-of-how-the-jeopardy-winning-supercomputer-was-born-and-what-it-wants-to-do-next/

Google Brain: https://www.wired.com/2012/06/google-x-neural-network/

Stanford University study:
https://ai100.stanford.edu/sites/default/files/ai_100_report_0831fnl.pdf

AI jobs: http://www.economist.com/news/leaders/21701119-what-history-tells-us-about-future-artificial-intelligenceand-how-society-should

Chapter 2

AI Definition: http://searchcio.techtarget.com/definition/AI

Four AI types: http://www.livescience.com/56858-4-types-artificial-intelligence.html

Robot self-awareness: http://www.sciencealert.com/a-robot-has-just-passed-a-classic-self-awareness-test-for-the-first-time

Machine capabilities: http://simplicable.com/new/types-of-artificial-intelligence

Robot onslaught: https://qz.com/940977/no-one-is-prepared-to-stop-the-robot-onslaught-so-what-will-we-do-when-it-arrives/

AI industry growth data: https://www.techemergence.com/valuing-the-artificial-intelligence-market-2016-and-beyond/

Weber Shandwick study: http://www.webershandwick.com/uploads/news/files/AI-Ready-or-Not-report-Oct12-FINAL.pdf

Accenture: https://www.accenture.com/us-en/artificial-intelligence-index

KPMG: https://assets.kpmg.com/content/dam/kpmg/pdf/2016/04/employees-an-endangered-species.pdf

Startups: https://www.cbinsights.com/blog/artificial-intelligence-startup-funding/

Nvidia: http://www.nvidia.com/object/gpuventures.html

Consumer Brands & AI: http://www.adweek.com/digital/5-bleeding-edge-brands-are-infusing-retail-artificial-intelligence-175312/

Amazon: https://techcrunch.com/2016/11/30/amazon-launches-amazon-ai-to-bring-its-machine-learning-smarts-to-developers/

Watson & Salesforce: http://www.cnbc.com/2017/03/06/ibm-and-salesforce-shake-hands-on-artificial-intelligence.html

Self-service data: http://www.techrepublic.com/article/5-big-data-trends-that-will-shape-ai-in-2017/

Chapter 3

AI Education: https://www.ft.com/content/5bf845fe-b7c2-11e6-961e-a1acd97f622d

Job trends: http://www.bbc.com/news/technology-34066941

Automation Potential: http://www.mckinsey.com/business-functions/digital-mckinsey/our-insights/where-machines-could-replace-humans-and-where-they-cant-yet

Chapter 4

Jason Alan Snyder article: http://www.adweek.com/digital/4-ways-catch-robots-attention-your-marketing-168790/

Survdata: https://www.survata.com/capabilities/

Mariana: https://www.marianaiq.com/

Swarm AI: http://www.techrepublic.com/article/how-to-use-swarm-a-i-instead-of-polls-for-market-research/

Watson & Lucy: https://www.wsj.com/articles/ibm-watsons-data-crunching-gains-traction-with-marketing-firms-1463569201

Perception of AI: https://hbr.org/2016/10/what-do-people-not-techies-not-companies-think-about-artificial-intelligence

AI & Brand Marketing: http://adage.com/article/cmo-strategy/marketers-ai-improve-brand-experience/306483/

GeoMarketing 101: http://www.geomarketing.com/geomarketing-101-internet-of-things

Location-based marketing: https://bluedotinnovation.com/location-services-2017-top-predictions.html

Amazon recommendations: http://fortune.com/2012/07/30/amazons-recommendation-secret/

HubSpot Academy: http://academy.hubspot.com/

Salesforce certification: https://www.salesforce.com/form/services-training/certification-journey-ebook.jsp

Natural Language Generation: https://www.narrativescience.com/Resources/Resource-Library/Article-Detail-Page/what-is-natural-language-generation

Wordsmith: https://automatedinsights.com/wordsmith

Quill: https://www.narrativescience.com/Platform

AI & Presentations: https://www.fastcompany.com/3064951/can-these-ai-powered-tools-help-you-perfect-your-next-presentation

Linking human brains to AI: http://fortune.com/2017/04/21/elon-musk-neuralink-brain-machine/

Facebook brain recognition: https://www.recode.net/2017/4/19/15361568/facebook-mark-zuckerberg-brain-mind-reader-regina-dugan-building-f8

Social AI: https://venturebeat.com/2017/02/07/what-social-artificial-intelligence-means-for-marketers/

AI-produced art: http://www.hodlipson.com/robotic-art.html

AI web design: http://www.huffingtonpost.com/harold-stark/worlds-collide-artificial_b_11664470.html

Retail brands & AI: http://www.adweek.com/digital/5-bleeding-edge-brands-are-infusing-retail-artificial-intelligence-175312/

Logojoy: https://www.logojoy.com/

MarkMaker: http://emblemmatic.org/markmaker/#/about

Co.Design critiques design automation: https://www.fastcodesign.com/3058852/what-happens-when-you-apply-machine-learning-to-logo-design

Google captioning AI: https://petapixel.com/2016/09/23/googles-image-captioning-ai-can-describe-photos-94-accuracy/

CaptionBot: https://www.captionbot.ai/

Google Quick Draw: https://quickdraw.withgoogle.com/
AutoDraw: https://aiexperiments.withgoogle.com/autodraw

Limits to creative AI: https://hbr.org/2017/04/there-will-always-be-limits-to-how-creative-a-computer-can-be

PR & AI: http://www.prnewsonline.com/its-time-for-pr-to-embrace-artificial-intelligence/

News: http://www.journalism.org/2016/05/26/news-use-across-social-media-platforms-2016/

News writing: https://www.wired.com/2017/02/robots-wrote-this-story/

JUICE: http://jlab.uib.no/2016/06/13/juice-innovative-search-engine-for-journalists/

PR Tools: https://blog.hubspot.com/agency/pr-tools#sm.0001azd8ofuo7dxixt92ninq1718a

Disney MagicBand: https://www.wired.com/2015/03/disney-magicband/

AI-powered Disney robots: http://www.access-ai.com/news/664/disney-to-use-ai-to-bring-robotic-characters-to-life-at-theme-parks/

AI-powered events: http://www.eventmanagerblog.com/artificial-intelligence-infographic

AI-powered purchasing: http://www.adaptation-inc.com/future-of-procurement-is-digital/?platform=hootsuite

Chapter 5

Bot support perception https://venturebeat.com/2016/09/05/the-chatbot-revolution-in-customer-support/

Human touch: http://www.huffingtonpost.com/entry/ai-powered-customer-service-needs-the-human-touch_us_58b88046e4b0ffd61787bd3d

Enterprise customer service:
https://www.forbes.com/sites/adelynzhou/2017/02/27/how-artificial-intelligence-is-transforming-enterprise-customer-service/#1a0ec48a14836
Oracle whitepaper:
https://www.oracle.com/webfolder/s/delivery_production/docs/FY16h1/doc35/CXResearchVirtualExperiences.pdf

Salesforce & service: https://techcrunch.com/2017/02/13/salesforce-brings-ai-to-service-cloud/

Chapter 6

Endangered occupations:
https://www.forbes.com/sites/bernardmarr/2016/04/25/surprisingly-these-10-professional-jobs-are-under-threat-from-big-data/#6b2a73c57426

Augmentation:
https://automatedinsights.com/blog/tom_davenport_augmentation

Marketo AI perspective: http://blog.marketo.com/2017/03/marketing-and-artificial-intelligence-make-your-job-robot-proof.html

Chapter 7

Agent: https://quizlet.com/12032652/robots-expert-systems-and-artificial-intelligence-vocab-flash-cards/

Turing Test: http://www.bbc.com/future/story/20150724-the-problem-with-the-turing-test

Accenture on AI: https://www.accenture.com/us-en/artificial-intelligence-index

AI Trends: https://aitrends.com/

Practical Artificial Intelligence for Dummies:
http://gunkelweb.com/coms493/texts/AI_Dummies.pdf

Intel Nervana AI Academy:
http://www.intel.com/content/www/us/en/analytics/artificial-intelligence/overview.html

TopBots: http://www.topbots.com/

Stanford University Machine Learning course:
https://www.coursera.org/learn/machine-learning
Class Central AI course catalogue: https://www.class-central.com/subject/ai

theONswitch: http://www.theonswitch.com

ai world conference: https://aiworld.com/

O'Reilly Artificial Intelligence Conference:
https://conferences.oreilly.com/artificial-intelligence/ai-ny

Chapter 8

2001 A Space Odyssey: https://www.wired.com/2015/08/amazingly-accurate-futurism-2001-space-odyssey/

Ex Machina: http://www.imdb.com/title/tt0470752/

RoboCop: http://www.imdb.com/title/tt0093870/

Human-powered reviews of AI films:
https://www.cnet.com/pictures/hollywood-ai-16-films-artificial-intelligence/

Twilight Zone episode: http://www.imdb.com/title/tt0734633/

Star Trek episode: http://www.imdb.com/title/tt0708481/

Build your own robot: http://www.robotshop.com/

Retro robot accessories: http://www.retroplanet.com/CTGY/Robots.html

About the Author

theONswitch: http://www.theonswitch.com/

Don't Hook Up With the Dude in the Next Cube:
https://www.amazon.com/Dont-Hook-Dude-Next-Cube/dp/0982755422

About Jim D'Arcangelo

VentureBeat Webinar: https://venturebeat.com/2017/03/30/its-time-marketing-went-all-in-on-machine-learning-and-ai-vb-live/

Made in the USA
San Bernardino, CA
03 August 2018